STEP-UP
ART AND DESIGN

People in Action

Susan Ogier

Evans

Published by Evans Brothers Limited
2A Portman Mansions
Chiltern Street
London W1U 6NR

© Evans Brothers Limited 2009

Produced for Evans Brothers Limited by
White-Thomson Publishing Ltd,
Bridgewater Business Centre,
210 High Street,
Lewes, East Sussex BN7 2NS

Printed in Hong Kong by New Era Printing Co. Ltd

Project manager: Rachel Minay

Designer: Leishman Design

The right of Susan Ogier to be identified as the
author of this work has been asserted by her in
accordance with the Copyright, Designs and
Patents Act 1988.

British Library Cataloguing in Publication Data

Ogier, Susan

People in Action – (Step-up Art & Design)
1. Art and design – Juvenile literature
I. Title
372.5'2

ISBN-13: 978 0237 535 780

Acknowledgements:

Special thanks to Mrs Pat Allen and the teachers
and pupils in Years 3, 4, 5 and 6 at St Luke's
Primary School, Kingston upon Thames, Surrey,
for all their artwork and help in the preparation
of this book.

Picture acknowledgements:

Alamy: page 26t (David Pearson). Bridgeman Art
Library: pages 5t (Louvre, Paris, France, Giraudon),
6 (Musee Rodin, Paris, France, Giraudon), 8
(Museum of Fine Arts, Houston, Texas, USA, Gift of
Audrey Jones Beck), 22b (National Gallery, London,
UK), 24b (Victoria & Albert Museum, London, UK),
25t (Museum of Fine Arts, Houston, Texas, USA,
Gift of Mrs Eleanor Freed). Corbis: pages 7t
(Kazuyoshi Nomachi), 10b (Alinari Archives), 12,
14t (Burstein Collection), 14b (National Gallery
Collection. By kind permission of the Trustees of the
National Gallery, London), 16 (National Gallery
Collection. By kind permission of the Trustees of the
National Gallery, London), 18 (David Pollack), 20
(National Gallery Collection. By kind permission of
the Trustees of the National Gallery, London), 23
(Francis G. Mayer), 26b (Burstein Collection). Chris
Fairclough: cover (main), pages 7b, 9b (both), 11,
13t&b, 17l, 19, 21b, 25b, 27b, 28r, 29r. Bella
Horwood: page 15. Istockphoto: cover tl (Justin
Horrocks), cover tr, pages 4l, 5br (all), 21tl&r, 28l,
29l. The National Portrait Gallery: page 27t.
Popperfoto: page 4r. Shutterstock: title page
(Christophe Testi), pages 5bl, 9t (Christophe Testi),
10t, 17c&r, 22t (all), 24t.

Contents

Investigating movement

All living things are able to move. Humans can move because of our system of muscles and bones working together.

Life processes

Movement is one of the seven life processes that all living things have in common. Do you know what the other six are? You might have learned the mnemonic 'MRS GREN'.

Movement and muscles

The human skeleton is the framework of bones that supports the body and protects its delicate organs, such as the brain and the heart. Bones are attached to muscles. Bones can only move when the brain tells the muscles to pull them.

Try to feel the muscles working as you move an arm or leg. There are about 650 muscles in a human body and you can keep yours healthy by doing exercise or sport.

▶ *Look at this picture of the athlete Kelly Holmes. Can you see how well defined her muscles are? Exercise makes our muscles bigger and stronger.*

Art and science

Artists were the first people to record the structure of the human body. Leonardo da Vinci, a famous artist, scientist and engineer, made detailed drawings in 1510 that showed how muscles and bones work.

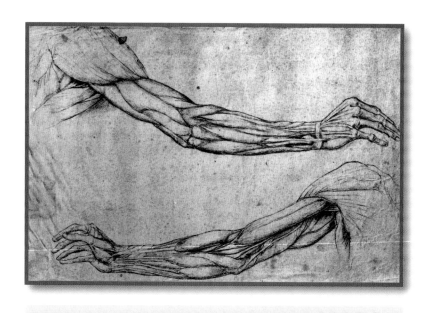

▶ *This drawing by da Vinci shows the muscles and tendons in the arm. Tendons are strong cords that attach muscles to bones.*

Ways of moving

Consider all the different ways the human body can move. Think about small movements, such as blinking an eye or wiggling a toe, as well as ones like running or jumping. List some words that describe the movements, for example quiet, flowing or dynamic.

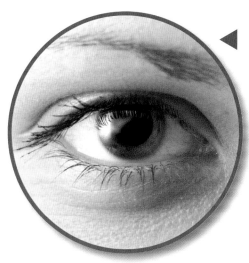

◀ *The eye muscle is the fastest reacting muscle in the human body. A person blinks, on average, about 15,000 times a day.*

Collecting information

Look in magazines, newspapers and comics for pictures of people making movements, and collage them in your sketchbook. What are the figures doing in the pictures? Can you still tell what movement they are making once you have cut them out, or did the background give you extra clues?

Drawing movement

There are many different ways to show people in action through art. One way is to concentrate more on the movement than on the figure, although the figure might seem to be 'alive' through the use of this technique.

▶ *In this drawing, Cambodian Dancer, we can see how the artist, Auguste Rodin, is interested in the gestures made by the dancer during the dance. Rodin has not even attempted to get a likeness of his model because the movement, not the person, is the important thing here.*

Mark-making

To be able to represent movement itself you have to re-learn to scribble. Try using some charcoal to make marks on a large sheet of paper. Think of the words you used to describe ways of moving on page 5 and then use your charcoal to describe these words in a visual way. For instance, make your mark run, jump, skip, zoom or slide. What else did you come up with?

Charcoal

Charcoal has one of the longest histories of all artists' materials as it was used to make cave paintings 30,000 years ago. Charcoal is made by burning wood very slowly – it takes about three whole days to turn a piece of wood into charcoal.

▶ *Even in prehistoric times, artists were interested in capturing movement in a visual way. They might have been reflecting the fact that people needed to catch fast-moving animals in order to feed themselves and their families.*

Communicating movement

Work with a partner, taking turns to move constantly while the other is drawing. Make sure you are not trying to draw the person that you know, but the movement and gestures that he or she is making. Use charcoal and chalk to create marks that suggest the motion, perhaps by using flowing, expressive lines. It can be very exciting to work at this speed. Try to think about the decisions you are making while drawing.

▶ *Nisha has used charcoal and carefully torn pieces of collage to show the motion of the model that she was drawing. Like Rodin, she has used expressive lines to show movement.*

Pin your work up and stand back to look at it. Do the drawings express the idea of movement? What would you do differently if you could do this again?

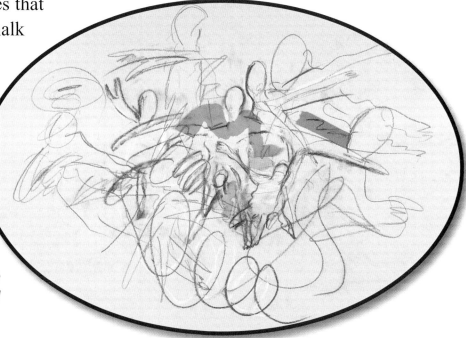

Dance and music

We have seen how artists use marks to express gesture, and these techniques can also be used to show rhythm, dance and music in an artwork.

The Impressionists

The Impressionists were a group of artists who were interested in trying to show movement in their work. One of the ways that they did this was by choosing subjects that were *about* movement, and by trying to capture the actual moment that the movement took place on the canvas. Impressionist art gives us an 'impression' – rather than a photographic-style representation – of the action that is taking place.

Experiments

Edgar Degas was an Impressionist artist who was famous for painting dancers and circus performers. Degas was very experimental with the materials he used in his paintings.

For instance, he might use soft pastels with rags and water to create different effects.

▲ *This lively picture is Russian Dancers by Edgar Degas. Degas has layered colours in pastels to create a sense of movement. Imagine what music might be playing and which instruments are being used. Do you think that the music would be fast or slow?*

Playing with pastels

Make your own experiments with soft and oil pastels in your sketchbook. In pencil, mark out some boxes across two pages and see if you can use the pastels in a different way in each one.

Indian classical dance

Watch some video clips of colourful dancers from India (see http://www.rajaradhareddy.com/production.html) and think about how you might make an impressionistic painting of them with pastels, using some of the techniques that you have discovered. Look at the shapes the dancers make with their bodies and how they move around the floor.

Look back at Degas' painting of Russian dancers to see how he used light and dark areas to help emphasise the movement. How could you incorporate this in your own work?

▲ This dancer is performing in the open air, perhaps at a street festival. Can you imagine some of the sounds that you might hear if you were standing watching this? Perhaps you could play some Indian music while you are working on your pastel picture to help inspire you.

◄ These artworks are made with soft pastels, like much of the work by Degas. The bright colours used reflect the vibrant costumes of the Indian dancers.

Speed

Artists are always experimenting with new ways of working. Today there are many techniques and materials in new media, such as digital cameras and videos, that are able to represent fast movement.

Technology and art

Technology is always advancing and artists can use these new technologies to work in new ways. Some artists might also use their art to say something about the way technology is changing the world.

The Futurists

In the early 1900s, a group of Italian artists called the Futurists became fascinated with the industrial world and the power of technology over nature. The Futurists completely rejected the ideas of the past, especially ideas to do with art. They were interested in speed and movement, and their subjects included cars, trains, planes and electricity.

▲ Modern technology allows us to live our lives at a fast pace. How has the camera captured the movement of people in this busy railway station?

◄ This sculpture is by Umberto Boccioni, one of the Futurists. It is called Unique Forms of Continuity in Space. A bronze sculpture like this stays in one place, so how has the artist conveyed a sense of movement?

Speed and sport

Watch other children in the school grounds as they are running, playing or taking part in a football or netball match. What kinds of movements do you notice? Make some thumbnail sketches with a soft pencil in your sketchbook and take digital photographs of some of the actions.

Work with a partner to make more detailed drawings of some of the movements you observed. Take turns to hold the pose while the other draws. You could use a combination of drawing materials, such as charcoal, chalk and pastels. Try blurring the edges of your drawings to give the impression of speed and movement.

Transformation

Develop this idea by making some sculptures out of cardboard using Boccioni's example as a starting point. How will you transform the figures into abstract shapes that will show movement? Use your own drawings and photos to inspire you.

When you are happy with the shape of your sculpture, stand back and look at it from different angles. Does it need any additional work? You might like to paint it. Decide whether adding or taking something away is needed before it is finished.

◀ *Sculpture is all about 'form' and 'space', as suggested by the title of Boccioni's work. Children who were investigating these elements of art made sculptures by slotting cardboard shapes together. These sculptures were then painted with metallic poster paints.*

Film and photography

When we think of images of people in action, we probably first think of moving images. Today we are surrounded by the moving image via film and television, music videos, animated cartoons and computer games.

Lights, camera, action!

Find out all about films and make your own animation at:
http://www.filmstreet.co.uk

The first moving picture

In 1878, the photographer Eadweard Muybridge was the first person to find a way of stringing photographs together to make a moving image. Muybridge was challenged to prove whether a horse gallops with all four hooves off the ground at the same time. He set up a row of cameras that would take pictures in quick succession to try to capture this movement.

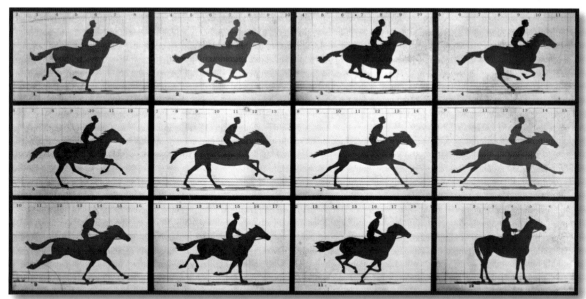

▲ *The pictures Muybridge took proved that a horse did lift all its hooves at once. They also showed that this happened when the legs were bent under the horse, rather than fully forward and fully back, as some artists had previously believed.*

Slow-motion study

Have you seen examples of actions being slowed down on film? Sometimes, sports television programmes use this technique to look carefully at the details of a goal in football, or to confirm the winner in a race.

Investigate this by making a slow-motion study in a PE lesson. Ask a friend to take digital photographs of you as you slowly change position. You might take a video film that you can watch on freeze-frame.

Use this information to make colour and tone studies by drawing contours of the moving

◀ How does this study show a sense of movement? How do the shades and contours help?

figure. To do this you could enlarge your photographs on the photocopier and use tracing paper to draw the outlines of the figures in their different positions. Transfer the outlined shapes to a larger piece of paper, overlapping some parts of the figures as you work across the page. Mix your own colours using delicate watercolours and fill in the body shapes, varying the tones where the shapes overlap.

You might develop this further by working with a group of friends to make a large-scale version that could be displayed in the gym.

Pose and position

When we look at an image of a person, the person's pose or position may tell us immediately what he or she is doing.

Body language

The painting on the right is *The Tea* by Mary Cassatt. What do you think of the women's poses? Do they look relaxed, happy and enjoying their cup of tea? Or do you think that that their body language is telling us something different? Notice also what the two women are wearing. Do you think one of them is visiting the other?

▲ There is only tea for two in this picture, so why do you think both women are looking across the room rather than at each other? Looking very carefully at the positions of their bodies and facial expressions can give us lots of clues.

Figure drawing

For a lesson in figure drawing, go to:
http://www.artisancam.org.uk/flashapps/figureitout/

Rest and relxation?

Look at the people in this painting by Georges Seurat. Their relaxed poses tell us they are enjoying a lazy afternoon by the river. In fact, they are all workers from the factory in the background – this scene represents a break from their otherwise busy lives.

▲ Most of the men here are looking in one direction. Perhaps you could paint the view on the other side of the river.

Life models

When an artist is making an artwork that includes a figure, he or she might employ a life model to pose. Life models have to be able to stay very still in one position – without even scratching an itch – while the artist is working.

Sketchbook studies

Work with a partner on a series of poses and positions. Take it in turns to sit or stand in a pose while your partner makes a sketch. Can you think of some interesting poses? How long do you think you can hold a pose?

Photomontage

With a friend, use a camera to record several poses relating to a theme of your choice. For instance, you could use the painting *The Tea* as a starting point to investigate the sequence of actions that is necessary to make a cup of tea.

Make a montage with the sequence of photos and review the work with your friend. Does it tell the story that you intended it to? Perhaps you could write a set of instructions to go with your photomontage.

▶ *What story does this photomontage tell?*

Actions and emotions

Our emotions are an important part of who we are. How we feel inside can affect our body language and facial expressions. Think of some situations where you have felt strongly about something. Do you remember your first day of school? How do you feel on your birthday?

Emotions in art

We can often explore our own feelings, as well as recognising how others are feeling, by looking at works of art. Emotions that are portrayed in paintings can help us to understand what is happening in the picture, and what the artist's intention might have been.

Thinking and feeling

How do you feel when you are working on a piece of art? Do you feel excited when it is going well, and frustrated when it is not? Which of your senses encourages you to draw, paint or make something? Perhaps you could write down some of your thoughts in your sketchbook. Your sketchbook can become a place for you to record your thoughts and feelings, and somewhere for you to organise them into ideas for artwork – a bit like a diary.

► *This painting is called* An Experiment on a Bird in the Air Pump. *Look at the faces, as well as the positions, of the figures. What do you imagine each of these people is feeling?*

Mirror images

Make studies of facial expressions that show strong emotions in your sketchbook. Use a hand mirror to pull faces that show emotion and carefully observe the shapes on your face before you draw. You might notice the different muscles that are used in your face when you show one of the six basic human emotions: happiness, surprise, fear, sadness, disgust and anger.

Digital changes

Choose one emotion to explore more fully and have a digital photograph taken of you showing that emotion. Use a computer and software such as Photoshop to manipulate the image.

Try different effects to emphasise the emotion shown. Do any of the effects you try change the way your emotion might be understood?

Mixed media

Use photocopies of the printed-out photo to develop the idea further. Use a variety of different drawing and painting media, such as oil pastels, paint, marker pens, charcoal and chalk, on the separate images. Then make a display of all the faces. Which faces are really expressive? What impact do the multiple images have now that they are all together?

▼ *Which different emotions do these digital pictures show? Which image is your favourite, and why?*

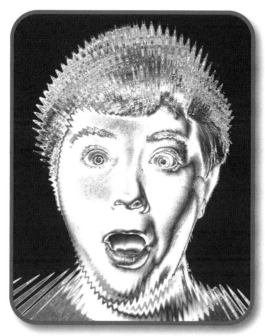

People in wartime

Although wars occur around the world today, we have not experienced one in our country since the 1940s. Your own grandparents or great-grandparents might remember the Second World War. Find out what life was like then for adults and children by looking at posters and other wartime art.

Poster art

Posters are created by graphic artists, who combine artwork with text in a way that is designed to be eye-catching. During the Second World War, posters carried simple but important messages to encourage the public to help the war effort.

Be bold

Create your own poster that tells the viewer what you feel passionate about. Perhaps, like the wartime artists, you want to encourage others to recycle, or save electricity by switching the lights off. Make your visual image bold and keep any text short and to the point to increase the impact of your message.

"OF COURSE I CAN!

I'm patriotic as can be—
And ration points won't worry me!"

▲ Everything was *rationed* during the Second World War. Posters like this one encouraged people to grow and preserve their own food.

Hard times

Visit the Imperial War Museum website (http://www.iwm.org.uk) to see war art and play the rationing game 'Make, Mend or Spend'.

War artists

During the Second World War, artists such as Henry Moore and John Piper were asked to make artwork of events that they witnessed. Piper's paintings give an impression of the devastation and sadness that war brings, by the use of dark tones and images of broken-down and bombed buildings. Henry Moore sketched people sleeping in the London Underground while they were sheltering from bombs.

Children's war

Investigate what life was like for children during the Second World War. You could read about Anne Frank or ask a relative to talk to your class about his or her real-life experience as an evacuee.

Responding through art

How must the young evacuees have felt when they were parting from their parents? Explore this by making a life-size painting of an evacuee.

Begin by using books and the Internet to research the style, colours and patterns of clothes children wore in the 1940s. Then ask a partner to draw around you on very large paper to create the outline of your evacuee.

Use charcoal and poster paint to show the physical features and clothes of your evacuee. Draw the facial expression to show emotion – for example sadness, worry or fear.

▼ *Each evacuee had to wear a luggage label with his or her name on. The children who made this painting wrote imaginary 'letters home' on large labels and attached these to their artwork.*

I rubbed charcoal into the background to make it look like a smoky station.

Portraying relationships

Many artists use portraits of two or more people together to explore the relationships between them. Perhaps one of the most common themes in art is the relationship between a mother and her child, or family relationships.

Family portrait

This portrait, *Family Group in a Landscape*, is by Frans Hals and was painted in 1647. It shows two parents sitting with their children around them. Can you see how the younger children are painted as though they are moving and wriggling around while the parents and the older children seem to be more still?

Notice where the different people are looking and what they are doing with their hands. What do these clues tell you about the relationships between this group of people?

▲ *Frans Hals, who painted this family group, is well known for the realism of his portraits. Here, he has captured his sitters' personalities by placing them in very natural poses.*

Data on family size

Do you know any families with as many children as there are in the portrait above? Survey the children in your class to collect data on family size. What would be the best way to record the data as you collect it? What sort of graph or chart will you use to show the results of your survey?

Investigation

Find more examples of pictures that show two or more people and glue them into your sketchbook. Write notes next to the pictures saying what you think the different relationships between the people are.

Creating a double portrait

Think about your relationship with a close friend or family member – you might share similar interests or have the same sense of humour. Perhaps you could work with your friend to compose a portrait that shows your relationship. What will you both be doing in the portrait? Think about the colours that you might use. How will you use the background to say something about your relationship?

▶ *What adjectives can you think of to describe the relationship shown in this double portrait?*

You could use a combination of different drawing and painting materials to make your work. Combining collage, oil pastels and paint or inks can make your work look interesting and lively. You might consider how to use the materials in different ways to show textures, such as smooth skin or spiky hair.

Put your work on the wall and look at it. Have the mixed media techniques that you've used helped to create a lively piece of work?

Every picture tells a story

It is natural to try to work out the story in a piece of art because we want to understand what we are looking at. The purpose of some paintings is to do just that – to tell a story.

Religious painting

In the past, before many people could read, paintings were an important way to teach people about religion. Churches would be brightly painted with stories from the Bible and people would 'read' these pictures in the same way that we read words.

▶ *Many churches continue to tell stories with their colourful stained-glass windows.*

Narrative painting

The art of telling a story in a painted image is known as 'narrative painting'. Sometimes the whole story is shown and sometimes a scene will inspire us to find out the whole story or use our imagination to fill in the gaps.

◀ *This is* The Execution of Lady Jane Grey *by Paul Delaroche. Jane was queen for only nine days. Discover her story at: http://www.ladyjanegrey.org*

What's the story?

This painting by Georges de La Tour is called *The Fortune Teller*, but look carefully to discover the real story. Notice the actions of all of the characters and where they are looking. Who do you think is in on the trick?

▶ *What would you do if you saw something like this happening? You could have a discussion about this at circle time.*

In the news

Imagine you are a newspaper reporter and want to write an article about the story shown in *The Fortune Teller*. What might the scenes before and after have been? Perhaps there were other witnesses that you could interview.

Use a video camera to make a short news item with a group of friends. Decide who will take the roles of newscaster, interviewer, eyewitness and victim. Write a script and rehearse before you film. You could edit your work on the computer and then watch it on the interactive whiteboard.

Drama

Work in groups to create a drama around the theft, by inventing personalities for the characters and exploring their relationships. You could perform this at a class assembly and ask other children to think about the issues that you have raised.

Learning about another culture

Looking at pictures of people from different parts of the world can help us to understand their history, traditions and way of life. This allows us to compare their lives to ours and see the differences and the similarities.

The floating world

Ukiyo-e is a genre of Japanese art that dates from the Edo period (1600–1867). Ukiyo-e means 'pictures of the floating world' or 'pictures of a life filled with pleasure' and it shows us a way of life that existed in Edo (present-day Tokyo) in the past.

▶ *Look at this picture of modern Tokyo. It gives an impression of busy people in a crowded city, surrounded by colour and noise. Compare it with the Ukiyo-e picture below of old Tokyo (then called Edo), which dates from 1827.*

◀ *How does this print, The Tea House at Edo, compare to The Tea on page 14? What do the pictures tell us about the different lifestyles of these women?*

Subject matter

City life and exciting activities, such as the theatre, were popular subjects for the Ukiyo-e artists. Just as we are interested in the lives of celebrities today, the artists from the Edo period in Japan also made actors and actresses part of their subject matter. Many of the prints were originally made as advertising posters for the very popular Kabuki theatre shows.

Printmaking

Do your own printmaking project by using polystyrene blocks for press printing. Use a sharp pencil to etch an image into the polystyrene. Next, roll black ink over the surface of the polystyrene and then make prints on to separate sheets of paper.

When the ink is dry, use watercolour to hand paint your prints. Try different colour combinations on the individual sheets that you have printed. Which one do you prefer, and why?

▼ *The Ukiyo-e artists are famous for using a wood block technique to produce prints. This print is of a Kabuki actor.*

Haiku

Haiku are short, simple poems that use 17 syllables over three lines in a 5-7-5 formation. You could write a haiku to display next to your hand-coloured print.

Oriental rice.

Sushi wrapped in soft seaweed.

Noodles piping hot.

A visit to a gallery

Although we are able to access almost any picture that we want today, by looking at books or on the Internet, there is nothing like seeing the original piece of art.

Size matters

When we look at a reproduction of an artwork in a book we might imagine how big the original piece might be, but it can be surprising to see the scale of a painting or sculpture. It might be much larger or smaller that we had thought. Whether the work has a frame or not will also make a difference to how we view it. Look at some reproductions of paintings to see if the frame has been included.

Up close

The techniques that have been used by the artist can also be seen much more clearly by looking closely at the original. Perhaps the artist has used paint very thickly to create texture, or has used a very small, thin brush to produce fine detail.

▲ *Compare the space inside a gallery to other public spaces. What difference do you notice about the size of the rooms and height of the ceiling? Think about how the works are displayed. Are they randomly placed or is there a theme?*

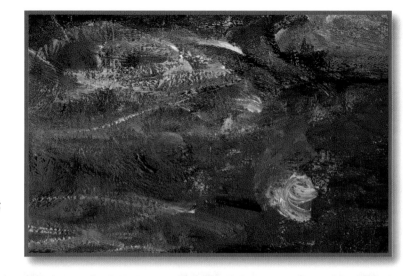

▶ *It is only when you get close to a painting that you can see the texture, patterns and layers of colour in the work. This close-up is from Monet's famous* Water Lilies *and the technique that he used looks surprisingly modern and abstract.*

A class visit

A Year 5 class visited the National Portrait Gallery in London as part of their history topic, The Tudors. They looked at this unusual portrait, *Sir Henry Unton*, which was painted in 1596 by an unknown artist. The portrait is unique in that it shows major events in Unton's life and makes much of his death, at the age of only 39.

▲ The tiny details in a painting like this would be hard to see in a reproduction so it was important for the children to see the portrait close up. The scenes shown include Henry's birth, education, marriage, travels, death and funeral.

▶ The children recreated scenes from the portrait during their class assembly.

Glossary

abstract   describes artwork that is not obviously a picture of something.

animated   appearing to move.

canvas   a strong woven fabric that is used as a support for oil or acrylic painting.

capture   to represent or record something.

charcoal   a material used for drawing, made by the slow burning of wood.

collage   to stick images or fabrics on to a flat surface to make an artwork. The finished artwork is also called a collage.

contour   the outline of a figure, body or object.

defined   showing an obvious outline.

dynamic   forceful or energetic.

etch   draw on to something by pressing or scratching into its surface.

evacuee   a person who has been removed (evacuated) from a dangerous place.

expressive   showing meaning or feeling, very clearly.

flowing   moving smoothly.

freeze-frame   a technique where a film is set on to 'pause'. This gives the impression of the stopped film looking like a still photograph.

genre   the category of a style of art.

gesture   the movement of a part of the body.

Kabuki   a type of Japanese theatre or drama, popular in the 17th century.

life model   a person whose job it is to pose for an artist.

life processes   all living things have seven processes in common: movement, reproduction, sensitivity, growth, respiration, excretion and nutrition.

likeness   a similarity in appearance.

medium   (plural **media**) a particular material or technique used by an artist.

mnemonic — a way of using a pattern of letters to help us remember something.

montage — an artwork made by placing many pictures or designs together.

oil pastel — a medium that has the texture of a wax crayon, but which allows colours to be blended more easily, especially when a little oil is added.

original — an original artwork is the one actually painted or made by the artist.

ration — to control how much of something people are allowed to buy.

reproduction — a replica or copy of an original artwork.

scale — relative size.

sketchbook — a plain paged book an artist uses to keep visual information to use another time. A sketchbook can be used for note taking, memory jogging, to solve problems or experiment with ideas and techniques.

soft pastel — a powdery, coloured art medium.

texture — the feel of a surface.

thumbnail sketch — a small, quick sketch, often made in preparation for a larger work.

tone — the lightness, darkness or quality of colour.

transform — to change in form or appearance.

viewer — the audience, or person, who is to look at the work.

wood block — a carved block of wood from which prints are made.

For teachers and parents

This book is designed to cover the learning objectives of the QCA Schemes of Work for Art and Design in KS2. Its aim is to provide imaginative and contemporary ways of working with the schemes. Specifically it covers Unit 6A People in Action, but essential elements of Unit 3A Portraying Relationships and the generic unit for years 3–6, Visiting a Museum, Gallery or Site, are also included.

Children may have already experienced Units 1A Self-Portrait and 2A Picture This! The ideas and activities are designed to act as starting points for deeper investigation and, in line with the programmes of study, it should be remembered that all the activities take place within the process of:

- Exploring and developing ideas.
- Investigating and making art, craft and design.
- Evaluating and developing work.
- Developing knowledge and understanding.

SUGGESTED FURTHER ACTIVITIES

Pages 4 - 5 Investigating movement
Art projects could link with investigations in science, for example Unit 5A Keeping Healthy or Unit 4A Moving and Growing, with PE and with issues that arise in PHSE such as 'living a healthy lifestyle'.

MRS GREN – the seven life processes are movement, reproduction, sensitivity, growth, respiration, excretion, nutrition.

One extension of the activity where children have made a collection of cut-out figures showing people moving would be to create a large collage that tells a story. This could be a collaborative project involving the whole class, or children could work in pairs. This could also be a springboard for creative writing.

Pages 6 - 7 Drawing movement
The scribbling activity is very useful for children whose drawings have become tight and worried. It can be used as a 'warming up' activity to prepare for large work. It is important to provide materials that encourage children to be free and experimental, especially when children are working in this way for the first time. Large sheets of cheap paper and charcoal, chalk, soft pastels or Chinese inks are ideal for working quickly.

For more information and images of Rodin's work go to: http://www.cantorfoundation.org/Rodin/rodin.html. An alternative is to look at the vibrant work of New York artist Keith Haring, which is full of movement and very appealing to children. Go to: http://www.haringkids.com/master_k_life.htm

Pages 8 - 9 Dance and music
The Impressionists were interested in capturing natural light and colour and the subtle changes that occur from one moment to the next. They loved to paint outdoors. Monet painted the same scenes many times but at different points in the day: http://giverny.org/monet/welcome.htm Demonstrate some Impressionist techniques, such as painting with strokes of unmixed colour, pointillist methods of applying colour and allowing the children to paint outdoors. Extend this by asking them to paint or take photos of the same scene at different times of the day, or over a longer period of time.

More video clips of Indian dancers are at: http://in.geocities.com/medhahari/bharata-natyam-bharathanatyam-bharatanatyam-bharatnatyam-videos.html. Perhaps you could ask an Indian dancer to come to your school to run a workshop. Extend the activity and explore the dance movements through sculpture, by making wire figures. Give the children flexible aluminium wire to create small sculptures that show how the body twists and moves when dancing. Make a base for each sculpture by stapling it to a piece of wood or MDF. Encourage the children to attach small sections of coloured tissue paper to their sculptures to represent the dancers' costumes.

Pages 10 - 11 Speed
Many of today's artists use video technology as a medium. Watch this artist's video with your class on the whiteboard, before trying your own speeded-up video experiments: http://www.videoart.net/home/Artists/VideoPage.cfm?Artist_ID=1781&ArtWork_ID=2127&Player_ID=9

Children can be helped to work quickly and on a small scale by using thumbnail sketches. Ask them to draw some boxes, or section off areas on a page in their sketchbooks; they can do one sketch in each box.

Using soft media such as chalk or pastels enables children to smudge the contours on their drawings to make them look blurred. This technique can give the effect of movement.

Pages 12 - 13 Film and photography

This website has interactive games that allow children to create and play back sequences of still photos: http://www.playingwithtime.org. Develop this idea by asking children to make a short film with their photos. They could use animation software on the computer and post the results on the school website. Children can make and publish their own animations at: http://fluxtime.com/eap1.php

Pages 14 - 15 Pose and position

The painting by Georges Seurat is *Bathing at Asnières*.

Drawing people can seem daunting, but for many artists this basic skill remains important. Children can be helped to draw a posed figure by first looking in great detail at their model. Encourage them to look at the large shapes that they see and draw those, rather than trying to put any detail in at this stage. Find imaginative ways to teach children how to look at and draw body shapes at: http://www.bartelart.com/arted/figure&portrait.html

Teach children to draw figures in various positions using the method on this website (which you can show on the whiteboard): http://www.alifetimeofcolor.com/main.taf?p=1,22. A good essay on how to teach children to draw is at: http://www.goshen.edu/art/ed/draw.html

Pages 16 - 17 Actions and emotions

Well-planned art activities can provide good opportunities for children to self-reflect and think about their feelings. This expectation can be introduced through looking at and talking about works of art that explore human emotions, such as Picasso's *Weeping Woman* (http://www.inminds.co.uk/weeping-woman-picasso-1937.html) or the works of Edvard Munch (http://www.edvard-munch.com/). The painting shown is by Joseph Wright of Derby and is at the National Gallery, London (http://www.nationalgallery.org.uk/). Allow children to have free access to their sketchbooks to make notes and to sketch their own private thoughts and ideas. For some, this will become a lifelong habit.

Pages 18 - 19 People in wartime

Link poster design to work in design and technology by taking children through the design process and evaluating the end product in terms of fitness for purpose.

For Henry Moore's emotive drawings go to: http://www.bbc.co.uk/schools/gcsebitesize/art/ao2/intentrev3.shtml and for the work of John Piper: http://collections.iwm.org.uk/server/show/conColObject.10986

For the evacuee activity, join four A1 sheets of white sugar paper together if you do not have poster sized paper. Wallpaper lining paper can also be used for any large-scale artwork.

Pages 20 - 21 Portraying relationships

Introduce and extend the suggested vocabulary from Unit 3A Portraying Relationships. Children could use words and phrases such as connection, emotional attachment, involvement, association, in a creative writing or poetry task on the theme of families or friendship.

A lesson plan for family portraits is at: http://www.artjunction.org/as_family.php

Look at the works of art suggested by the QCA scheme at the following weblinks: http://j9marshall.files.wordpress.com/2007/07/mr-and-mrs-clark-and-percy-hockney.jpg, http://www.artline.ro/admin/_files/photogallery/the_dance.jpg and http://www.abcgallery.com/V/vandyck/vandyck33.html

Pages 22 - 23 Every picture tells a story

Imagining the stories within paintings is one of the great pleasures of looking at works of art. It is important to choose examples that are interesting and engaging, and have the possibility of a range of interpretations. Notes on how to develop stories from art are at: http://www.smithsonianeducation.org/educators/lesson_plans/collect/telpai/telpai0a.htm and lesson plans from the Getty museum at: www.getty.edu/education/for_teachers/curricula/stories/

Children can find out about all sorts of stories in art at: http://cybermuse.gallery.ca/cybermuse/kids/stories/index_e.jsp

Pages 24 - 25 Learning about another culture

Find out about life in Japan as well as Ukiyo-e at: http://web-japan.org/kidsweb/
Learn about haiku at: http://www.gigglepoetry.com/poetryclass/Haiku.html

Pages 26 - 27 A visit to a gallery

Learning outside the classroom is an important aspect of children's educational experience. Find out about the resources and services available from your local gallery or museum and see where you can link a visit to one of these with your topic work. It may be possible to apply for financial help to cover the cost of coaches in order to transport children to cultural centres: http://www.grants4schools.info/portal/index.asp

Index